FUNNY THINGS
I SAID WHEN
I WAS FIVE

BY LEVI FISHER ROODENBURG

KR PUBLISHING

ISBN: 978-0-578-32576-7
Copyright 2021 by Kellen Roggenbuck
All Rights Reserved
Funny Things I Said When I Was Five
Written by Levi Fisher Roggenbuck

Levi is my son, and brings me laughs on a daily basis! I have taken the time to write down some of the shorter interactions to share with the world. It all started with a comment about nose rings that kept popping into my head days later and making me laugh out loud. After sharing the story on social media, it became obvious that other people found the moment as funny as well. I decided that it would be a tragedy for such profound, eloquent banter and musings to remain in our household alone. I am working within a supervisory role only, all conversations and quotes came directly out of Levi's mouth and mind, I just recorded them. As you will see, 5 years old is an odd age that has been amazing to witness and I hope you find more than a little joy in this book!

Sincerely,
Levi's Dad

Dad: How does it feel
being 5 now?
Levi: Good, now I can
be a boss.
Dad: Oh really?
Levi: Yes, I can tell you
what to do.
Dad: I don't think that's
how it works, bud.
Levi: Hmm, ask your boss
about that.
Dad: Who's my boss?
Levi: Me, weren't you
listening??

Levi: why is the police car
    turning there?
Dad: I think they are
    following that car.
Levi: oh, why?
Dad: I don't know.
Levi: maybe they live
    together?
Dad: you know what,
    maybe they do.
Levi: ...Do cats get married?
Dad: ...no.

Levi: Is that a mango forest?
Dad: It's a mangrove forest.
Levi: A mango forest?
Dad: Mangrove forest.
Levi: Mango?
Dad: Mangrove. MAN – GROVE.
Levi: MAN – GO.
Dad: No, mangrove trees.
Levi: Does it grow mangos?
Dad: Nope.
Levi: Oh. Does it drop seeds?
Dad: I guess so.
Levi:
Dad:
Levi: And do those grow into mangos?
Me: No mangos!

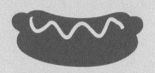

Levi: If you put the Lego hotdog
     stand sign on a truck, you
     have a hotdog truck.
Dad: That's true.
Levi: If you put it on the police
     station building, you got
     a hotdog station.
Dad: What's a hotdog station?
Levi: police serve you hotdogs.
Dad:
Levi:
Dad:
Levi: ...and probably spaghetti?
     Whatever you want.

"IF YOU
WINK
BOTH EYES,
THAT'S
SLEEPING."
:Levi

Levi: we need more
      cushions for our fort!
Dad: that's all we have,
      buddy.
Levi: then I'm going to
      make more cushions,
      I know how to!
Dad: oh yeah? How?
Levi:
Dad:
Levi: ...out of dog beds.

Levi: Dad, are there laws not in Jefferson?

Dad: There...are laws IN Jefferson.

Levi: What about stealing?

Dad: No stealing, that's against the law.

Levi: What if there were a store called "You Can Steal Everything"?

Dad: I don't think that would be stealing then.

Levi: But they say you can steal everything though.

Dad: I...think that's just giving you stuff.

Levi: Is it against the law?

Dad: I mean, no...because it's not stealing...

Levi: But that's the name of the store.

Dad: I understand, but stealing is taking without permission.

Levi: So it's not against the law?

Dad: Stealing is, yes.

Levi: But not having a store?

Dad:

Levi:

Dad: No it's not.

Levi: Good, I want a store.

?

Levi: Dad! I have no idea
        what is going on!
Dad: With what?
Levi: I don't know!
Dad: But...what makes you
        say that?
Levi: Because I don't know!
Dad: Yeah, but with what though?
Levi:
Dad:
Levi: I don't know, Dad.
Dad: Me...neither?

"I'm not being naughty, I'm a little boy."

:Levi

Levi (playing trains): Next stops South America, New York, Jefferson!

Dad: Ooh, the three big ones!

Levi: Yep!

Dad: How'd you choose those three stops?

Levi: What do you mean?

Dad: Like, how'd you choose where the train goes?

Levi: ...that's where the stops are.

Dad: Okay, but why did you choose those three places?

Levi ...that's where the stations are.

Dad:

Levi:

Dad: ...okay.

CRASH
Levi (from other room):
    Sorry, nothing!
Dad: What??
Levi: You didn't hear
    anything, right?
Dad: well, I heard that
    big crash...
Levi: NOTHING, RIGHT??
Dad:
Levi:
Dad: I mean, I think I did?
Levi: Nevermind, don't
    worry. Nothing!
    Trust me!
Dad: *sigh* okay.

Dad: Look! An airplane!
Levi: Yes! Let me know
    if you see any parrot
    shoes.
Dad: ...what?
Levi: What?
Dad: Do you mean 'parachutes'?
Levi: That's what I said.
Dad: I thought you said
    'parrot shoes'.
Levi: But what are parrot shoes?
Dad: I...I don't know...?

Levi: I think I need to call
    the Tooth Fairy.
Dad: Why??
Levi: I think it's funny when
    I drink water.
Dad: Are your teeth wiggly?
Levi: She needs to look at
    my teeth.
Dad: But are any wiggly?
Levi: Dad, please. Just call her.
Dad:
Levi:
Dad: ...I'll send her an email.

(While watching a video
about rollercoasters)
Levi: Wow! Can I go on that?
Dad: Yes, if you want.
Levi: Yes! I can hold my
      breath for a long time.
Dad: ...why do you need to
     hold your breath on
     a rollercoaster?
Levi: Because you wouldn't
      understand.
Dad:
Levi:
Dad: ...I don't understand.
Levi: I know.

Dad: If you could go
      anywhere right now,
      where'd you go?
Levi: I'd go to Jefferson.
Dad: You're already in
      Jefferson though.
Levi:
Dad:
Levi: Well, that was easy.

Levi: I think a storm
     is blowin' in.
Dad: You think so?
Levi: Yep, I can smell
     the weather.
Dad: What does it
     smell like?
Levi: *sniff*
Dad:
Levi: ...corn.

Dad: You can have French fries with
      that, if you want.
Levi: Really?!
Dad: Yes, are you excited?
Levi: I bet they are going to taste
      curly!
Dad: taste curly?
Levi: ...like my hair.

Dad: What do you want to
    play now?
Levi: How about I ride on your
    back like you are a
    horse?
Dad: How about I ride on
    YOUR back like you're a
    horse?
Levi:
Dad:
Levi: Are you making a joke?
Dad: Yes.
Levi: Oh...aren't jokes funny?
Dad: Apparently not when
    you're a dad.

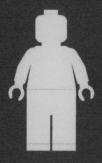

Dad: Hey, let's pick up some of
these toys.
Levi: (picks up the toys and
holds them)
Dad: Okay, good...now put
them away.
Levi: I can't do everything, Dad.
Dad: But...you have them in
your hands?
Levi: All I mean is you can help
some too.
Dad:
Levi:
Dad: ...I don't even know
where to begin.

Levi: (pretending to take a picture)
     hey Dad, smile for the picture!
Dad: *smiles*
Levi: No, maybe less smile...

Dad: do you think that steam is hot or cold?

Levi: I think it's...spoiling hot!

Dad: it's 'boiling hot' though.

Levi: what?

Dad: the phrase is 'boiling hot'.

Levi: No, I said spoiling hot.

Dad: I know buddy, but that's not right.

Levi: Oh...then I think it's spoiling cold.

Levi: That person has an earring in her nose.

Dad: Actually that's a nose ring.

Levi: ...what's a nose ring?

Dad:

Levi:

Dad: ...an earring in your nose.

Levi: Dad, when am I going to
      learn how to leap?
Dad: leap? Like jump?
Levi: yeah, when am I going to
      learn?
Dad: I don't know, I can teach
      you now maybe?
Levi: well... Maybe I'll wait to learn
      in school.
Dad: what?? Don't you think I can
      leap?
Levi:
Dad:
Levi: ...let's go color something
      maybe instead.

Levi: I'm going to jump on that, okay?
Dad: No! That would break it.
Levi: Aww, please??
Dad: Nope, if you broke that I'd be mad,
      it's brand new.
Levi: More mad than if I broke the toilet?
Dad: What? What's wrong with the toilet?
Levi: I didn't break it.
Dad: Then why'd you bring that up?
Levi: Just don't worry about it.
Dad: Just don't break anything!
Levi: I haven't yet.
Dad:
Levi:
Dad: what's "yet"?
Levi: I'm going to jump on that, okay?
Dad: NO!

Dad: What's your favorite animal?

Levi: Lion!

Dad: Why's that?

Levi: Because it starts with my favorite letter, 'L'.

Dad: Any other reason?

Levi: Their hair is in my favorite place, around their head!

Dad: I guess that's...

Levi: And their butts.

Dad: ...true.

Dad: What's it like being 5?
Levi: Good, and how old will
    I be next?
Dad: 6.
Levi: And then what?
Dad: 7...
Levi: and then?
Dad: 8.
Levi: And then?
Dad: 9.
Levi what then?
Dad: Okay, that's enough.
Levi: Oh, you don't know?
Dad:
Levi:
Dad: *sigh* 10.
Levi: ...and then what?

Levi: Dad, how old are you?
Dad: 37.
Levi: 3000?!
Dad: No, I'm 37.
Levi: 3000 is a good number,
      congratulations!
Dad: Okay, but that's not -
Levi: Happy birthday!
Dad: but...today's not...
Levi:
Dad: Okay, thanks.

"DAD, YOU MIGHT HAVE FORGOT, I CAN'T SEE IN THE DARK."

:Levi

Dad: hey bud, we should start
thinking about what you
want to get your mom for
Christmas.
Levi: I already know, a Lego train.
Dad: no, for you to give to mom
as a present. What do you
think she'd like?
Levi: um... Probably radishes.
Dad:
Levi:
Dad: like, a bag of radishes?
Levi: you know, for salads.
Dad: maybe we keep thinking.

Levi: (pointing to cartoon)
    Is that a taco?
Dad: Yep!
Levi: Is that it's belly
    button?
Dad: ...could be?
Levi: I bet it smells.
Dad:
Levi:
Dad:
Levi: ...like tacos.

(Driving in the truck)
Levi: Dad, when I'm older
      I'm going to drive the truck
      and Alivia is going to sit
      next to me.
Dad: Oh yeah?
Levi: Yes, and you will ride in
      the back on the way to
      the cemetery.
Dad: Why would we go to the
      cemetery?
Levi: Because you will be
      older then.
Dad: But why would we go to
      the cemetery??
Levi: I mean...I don't know...

Levi: Those squirrels are
     in my favorite tree!
Dad: you can share it.
Levi: Is that an oak tree?
Dad: Nope, it's a pine tree.
Levi: Yeah, but a pine
     oak tree?
Dad: No, just a pine tree.
Levi: ... But, like, an oak
     one?
Dad:
Levi:
Dad:
Levi: Squirrels like oaks.

Levi: Dad! Knock knock!
Dad: Who's there?
Levi: Um...cat!
Dad: Cat who?
Levi: Cat's got a fish face!
Dad: That's silly, what does
      it mean?
Levi: It's a joke.
Dad: Right, but what's it mean?
Levi: It means I'm funny.
Dad:
Levi:
Dad: But...
Levi: When you're funny, you'll
      understand, don't worry.
Dad: ...alright.

Dad: Levi, we're doing a
    bath tonight.
Levi: Okay Dad!
Dad: And we're going to
    have to wash your hair...
Levi: I don't think I can do
    that.
Dad: Why is that?
Levi: I don't think I'll have
    enough time - I need
    to learn to juggle.
Dad:
Levi:
Dad: Not with dirty hair
    you're not.

"MMM! THIS DINNER DOESN'T TASTE LIKE ASH AT ALL!"

:Levi

Levi: (looking at
        Dad's tattoo)
        Is that Jesus?
Dad: Yes.
Levi: But why doesn't
        he have a hat?
Dad:
Levi:
Dad: ...Honestly, I
        don't know.

THE
END
(HAPPY BIRTHDAY LEVI!)

CPSIA information can be obtained
at www.ICGtesting.com
Printed in the USA
BVHW050938291121
622783BV00016B/456